2017 The MVP Year

5777 The Year of the Triple Crown

CAROLYN G. ANDERSON

2017 The MVP Year

Book #1 of **#My7Years** Series

Copyright © 2017 by Integrity Publications

Published by Integrity Publications, a division of Integrity Consulting Enterprise, LLC

Book Cover and Interior designed by Riley Press

Printed in the United States of America. All scripture quotations, unless otherwise indicated, are taken from the Holy Bible, New International Version®, NIV®. Copyright ©1973, 1978, 1984, 2011 by Biblica, Inc.TM Used by permission of Zondervan. All rights reserved worldwide. www.zondervan.com The "NIV" and "New International Version" are trademarks registered in the United States Patent and Trademark Office by Biblica, Inc.TM

Other scripture references are noted and were either taken from the MSG, KJV, NKJV or AMP versions of the Bible. Other references were noted within the text and will not have its own reference page. Let's begin!

Table of Contents

Dedication

This book is dedicated to you and your Destiny!

Prophetic Testimonials

When God's people need to hear a NOW word of the Lord, God sends Carolyn G. Anderson to let them know what He is saying for that season and time.

In 2017 The MVP Year, Carolyn brings forth the timing of the Lord when God will initiate 'the seven years of abundance as it was in the days of Joseph.

Carolyn is a Prophet who is compassionate, loving and anointed in this hour to bring forth the ministry of Royalty, Wealth and Health. This book is a must for those who have an ear to hear and an eye to see what the Spirit of the Lord is saying NOW!

Apostle K. Anthony
Kingdom Cathedral International Ministries

I established some grand goals for the beginning of 2016 so I was excited to petition heaven for manifestation. During the midpoint of 2016, I felt stuck. I decided to multi task by praying and doing my required work. I told God that I needed to hear a word from Him because I felt stuck.

When I got off work, I received a call from Prophet Carolyn telling me that she had a word for me. She shared a word that equipped and empowered me to move from feeling unstuck to ready to possess the land that God promised me. She is an on-time Prophet.

Latreeta Burns
Jericho Church Without Walls

Background Information

HAPPY 2017!

The Prophetic calling on Carolyn's life can be traced back to her childhood. She was very discerning and oftentimes would know something was going to happen before it did. She would choose her friends wisely because God revealed the intentions of their hearts towards her and therefore she knew the right friends to hang around.

Subsequently, she made very wise choices because she could envision the results. There are very specific moments where Carolyn recalls making decrees (back then she just spoke not realizing what she was doing), about things to come in her life. There's one very specific moment in high school, where she told one of her best friends at the time that Kevel (husband now) would be her husband within 10 years. She wasn't interested in him at that time not even as a boyfriend. It would so happen that ten years later, Kevel became her husband and still is to this day. There are numerous accounts where she would know specific dates and times of events including the birthdates of her children, prior to the occasion.

The prophetic calling on her life truly gave birth on 3.1.03, where she had an encounter with God and He blessed her with the gift of speaking in tongues and the prophetic anointing.

It was from that moment that she would begin to flourish and realize that God speaks to her in various ways, especially through the alphanumeric language, nature, and blessed her with the gift to understand times and seasons. She also has the gift of wealth, healing and being very strategic.

To thresh the gift, she and her husband were both ordained as Apostles and Prophets and lead a Global Ministry that's transforming lives.

Most recently, God has given Carolyn very specific dates and times for the body so that they can understand His plans and purposes for their lives. Allow the message within this book to speak to you so that you can participate in God's timing and season.

The **TIME IS NOW!** It is the appointed time to begin your new journey and start fresh. Therefore, meet the **Fresh Voice** that God is using for such a time as this.

Introduction

Welcome to God's reset and the re-start of **the SEVEN YEARS of ABUNDANCE** as it was in the days of Joseph the dreamer as written in Genesis 41:29 NIV *"Seven years of great abundance are coming..."* It's the year of **MANIFESTATIONS, VICTORIES** and the re-establishment of your **PURPOSE** and many **PROMISES** being fulfilled. It's the year of the **MVP**.

For the past 14 years, I have been seeking God prior to the beginning of each new year for a theme or scripture for that year for me and my family. He was always faithful to give me a specific theme and our lives were guided that year concerning the vision for that year. When my husband and I started Pastoring in 2011, we sought the Lord even further for a theme for the ministry. In addition to the general word for the church, each member received personal prophetic ministry concerning their lives. At this same time, we also started learning more about our Messianic Jewish roots and about God's biblical calendar, which is different from the Gregorian/Julius calendar. Most people are familiar with the Gregorian calendar as it's the most observed and widely printed.

Nevertheless, with the new knowledge of God's calendar, we started living according to both calendars, except our celebrations,

15

observations, feasts and times of fasting are according to God's calendar. During very specific appointed times with God, He revealed to me that He elevated me from being just a Prophet that minister's personal prophecies, to a Prophet on a Global basis that understands His timing and season and was a strategic voice that transform lives. From then leading up to today, I have been declaring the meaning of the YEARS and what God has in store for His people. It's time to get excited as you are about to receive many things that you have been hoping for. Your dreams are about to become a reality.

It's time for **MANIFESTATIONS** in your life. The time has come for your Goals, Dreams and Desires to begin to come to fruition in 2017. You will see the Word of God come alive in your life. You are the **Most Valuable Player** in your game of life and you must out play your opponent so that you get the victory.

It's the year of **VICTO (RIES)** and the Year of the Re's. There shall be many **Victories**, such as **Miracles and Healing**, **Wealth Transfer**, and a **re-pay** for what you've lost in previous years. It is also the year of the **Triple Crown** and the beginning of the **seven years of abundance**. Get ready to walk in wealth and royalty. It's your TIME, claim it, believe it and receive it. God will perfect some things in you and complete some things that He already started.

It is the Year to truly walk out your **PURPOSE**. This is not the year to be a replicable of somebody else or to be a carbon copy of another person's vision. You will truly need to know your purpose in life and what you were created to be and to do. The late Dr. Myles Munroe said, **"The greatest tragedy in life is not death, but life without meaning, without a purpose."** Therefore, it's time to truly live life with meaning. You will need to know where you fit in, within the seven spheres of influence, also referred to as the seven mountains. Are you called for your purposes to be established in **Business, Media, Family, Arts & Entertainment, Ministry, Government and/or Education?** Sometimes you are called to more than one, but know at least which one you'll occupy until He returns.

Dr. Myles Munroe (1992) also said "fulfillment in life is dependent on becoming and doing what one was born to be and do. **Anything less makes life an enemy and death a friend.**" It is essential, vital, crucial and necessary that there's understanding of the fundamental principle of purpose and pursue it wholeheartedly. For without purpose, life has no direction and those who don't know where they are going will probably end up someplace else.

Don't end up being one of those men and women who die, never truly living their purpose. There are several graves with unfulfilled potential just lying dead. You are alive for such a time as

17

this, so activate your PURPOSE and walk it out. Ask God what is your purpose in life? He will answer you. If you need guidance to get started on understanding your purpose, you can find resources on my websites.
www.carolynganderson.com
http://transform.carolynganderson.com/

There are many **PROMISES** in your life yet to fulfilled. If you just open one of the books that is found in the blueprint for life (The Bible), you will see that God has promised you a great life. It's time for you to decree and declare those promises until they **MANIFEST**. The time is NOW! There are 77 decrees and declarations in this book that you can decree and declare over your life daily. Let this be one of the best years of your life. I am believing with you! You oversee your destiny based on the choices and decisions that you make daily, so choose wisely.

Purpose of the Book

This book is the first of seven books that's a part of the Prophetic Series called **#My7Years.** The purpose of the book is to share what God is doing right NOW! and what's to come. It's time for the people of God to participate in God's timing so that **His will** be done on earth as it is in Heaven. God has revealed part of His Sovereign plan to me and its imperative that you take hold of it as the time is NOW! According to Amos 3:7 NIV it says, ***"Surely the Sovereign Lord does nothing without revealing his plan to his servants the Prophets."*** Let the revelations flow to you as you read this book.

God has a set time for everything and He desires for us to be in sync with His timing so that we can truly live out our purpose and kingdom mandate. Thus, the purpose of the book is to let you know the timing of what God is doing and to share strategies on how to effectively activate your purpose. You become more effective when you understand what God is doing. It makes you wiser and makes the journey of life more pleasant to live. According to Psalm 90:12 NIV, it says ***"Teach us to number our days, that we may gain a heart of wisdom"*** and Job 14:5 NIV says ***"A person's days are determined; you have decreed the number of his months and have set limits he cannot*** *exceed."* Thus, knowing what season of life you are in and where you are going plays an intricate role in your destiny.

According to Ecclesiastes 3:1-8 NIV *"There is a time for everything, and a season for every activity under the heavens: a time to be born and a time to die, a time to plant and a time to uproot, a time to kill and a time to heal, a time to tear down and a time to build, a time to weep and a time to laugh, a time to mourn and a time to dance, a time to scatter stones and a time to gather them, a time to embrace and a time to refrain from embracing, a time to search and a time to give up, a time to keep and a time to throw away, a time to tear and a time to mend, a time to be silent and a time to speak, a time to love and a time to hate, a time for war and a time for peace."* The TIME to obtain Wealth, to see Manifestations, experience many Victories, Reset, live life on Purpose and seeing your Promises being fulfilled is NOW!

Chapter 1 – Spin Cycle

The year 2016 felt like a Spin Cycle. It was a year that had many ups and downs, trials and tribulations, some victories, and a feeling that words couldn't describe. This was because 2016 was a year when God was doing a reset. It started back in 2015, when many Prophets were ministering gloom and doom that was forthcoming on the earth. This was not accurate, because I knew that God had shared with me that we were getting ready to enter the season of Abundance as it was in the days of Joseph.

Therefore, God had to re-shuffle some things around and re-set some things and conduct a change in guards. So many Christians were experiencing trials and tribulations to the point where it felt as though God was sending judgement. It was not judgement, it was God sending a test to get us ready for the major changes. Many needed to get in position so that God could reveal His divine plan.

There were so many Christians that lost hope and some came to the verge of totally giving up. Perhaps you were one of them that felt like 2016 was a world-wind. One minute when it seems like things were going great, suddenly it was disappointment and brokenness. Just when things seemed hopeful, it was deferred. Some people literally became ill in their bodies while waiting for a change. According to Proverbs 13:12 NIV it states, *"Hope deferred makes the heart sick, but a longing fulfilled is a tree of life."* Therefore, God is getting ready to fulfill several promises in your life so that you can eat from the tree of life and experience His love.

God says those that are reading this book and have stood the test, get ready because your reward is at hand. The spin cycle was meant to squeeze out the last ounce of heaviness so that you could enter the new finishing cycle. God had to heal the wounds and is still healing some wounds, some deep soul issues, emotional issues, relational issues, brokenness, financial drought and some heavy burdens that you've been carrying.

Just like doing a load of laundry, there's a process that must take place to get to the finished product. There's a process to get the clothes clean and ready to wear again. This process of getting dirty laundry to clean clothes cannot be accomplished with just one equipment. It requires two equipment's, a washer and a dryer. God is saying that to succeed in this next seven years of blessings and abundance that's at hand, it will require divine alignments, strategic partnerships, unity and togetherness to thrive and be victorious.

Like any process there are steps that are necessary to have a quality product or result. Take for example the process of doing a load of laundry. It's a four-step process. First the clothes are washed, then rinse and finally the spin cycle. The spin cycle is the step before putting the clothes in the dryer to complete the steps that make the clothes wearable again. If the clothes are not removed after the spin cycle and placed in the dryer, they will begin to smell.

I've experienced this smell several times because I happen to be married to a man that constantly leaves his clothes in the washer. Unlike me, my husband doesn't do his laundry at one time. He oftentimes forgets that he started a wash cycle. Me on the other hand only do laundry if I know I have enough time to complete the entire process. I wash, dry and put the clothes away nice and warm.

There were few times that my husband had to go back through the wash cycle to remove the odor and smell from the clothes after being left in a washer for a while. Perhaps some of you have felt like you're being washed and washed and going through the same cycle all over again. Well it's time to put your faith into action and get ready because your (up and down) cycle is coming to an end.

If you feel like you've been in the spin cycle repeatedly, it's because God is still squeezing something out of you or it could be that you didn't complete a test or a process in its totality. Do an evaluation of your life and see where you are, today.

When the entire process is complete the dryer will make a sound. It's the sound that says, it's time, it's time, take me out because I'm refreshed and ready for the next level. It's time to wear the fresh clothes and walk out the new season.

Moments of Reflection..................

I want you to pause and take a moment and reflect on your life. Write out some new things or things you're going to do differently in 2017.

_____

_____

_____

_____

_____

_____

_____

_____

Chapter 2 - The Year 5777

Earlier, I shared about God's Biblical calendar and the Gregorian calendar, which is the one you're probably more familiar with. God established His biblical calendar so that the Children of Israel would remember Him and set aside certain times as appointed moments with Him. While we are no longer operating under the law of Moses, God's biblical calendar still exists.

There are certain set times that are days of observance and is also believed to be days that God does mass healing, blessings, forgiveness, and review the book of life. One of those appointed time is Rosh Hashanah (October 3, 2016) and Yom Kippur also known as The Day of Atonement (October 12, 2016). Rosh Hashanah is considered the Head of the Year or the Civilian New Year. It is believed to be the time that God made civilization (Adam and Eve). Therefore, every year around this time, the Jewish people and other Kingdom followers will observe that day and the 10 days of awe (Yom Kippur) thereafter, as a time of mourning and fasting. Yom Kippur is one of God's High Holy Days and is said to be the day that God forgives our sins and re-start our lives with His blessings.

Our immediate family celebrates Rosh Hashanah, Yom Kippur and the other appointed days to honor God and to show Him that we believe His Word and are participating with His time and season. We have seen tremendous blessings in our lives, since wholeheartedly following the Jewish Calendar. Observing the Sabbath Day and keeping it Holy is also one of the days that should be observed if you want to experience the blessings of the Lord in its fullness.

On October 2, 2016, Rosh Hashanah was the Jewish New Year 5777. The year 5777 is the year of the **Triple Crown**, the year of God **perfecting some things in us**, the year of completion (resets) and the year of **divine rest**. This is not a rest where you do nothing, but rather rest from the enemy.

As God's chosen people we get to celebrate three (3) New Years - Rosh Hashanah (typically September or October), January 1st and Nisan 1 (around March-April), which is the Biblical New Year- the time when the children of Israel had the Great Exodus from Egypt. The Jewish people celebrate this time also as a re-start of God's calendar.

Consequently, God said that this year He was establishing three major resets and they would fall within the timeframe of the 3-new year above.

"You are never too old to set another goal or to dream a new dream." C.S. Lewis

Moments of Reflection..................

Pause and take a moment to reflect: Write 7 Goals that you would like to accomplish this year.

_____

_____

_____

_____

_____

_____

_____

_____

_____

_____

_____

_____

_____

Chapter 3 – The Year 2017

Seventeen – the number of Victory

The number seventeen (17) has been associated with VICTORY. Before I did the research on the number 17, God revealed to me that 2017 was the year of many **VICTO-RIES (Re's),** such as re-set, re-demption, re-velation, re-newal, re-stitution and so on. He said many victories will **MANIFEST** in 2017. You have suffered and went through a lot in the past years and now it's time for a re-pay and a re-turn on your investments.

Back in September 2016, I started declaring the year of the Re's. Therefore, when I did my research on the number 17, it was only a confirmation for what God had already shared with me, during my sabbatical (in-time) with Him.

In the Bible the number 17 symbolizes "overcoming the enemy" and "complete victory." God overcame the sins of rebellious humans when he began to flood the earth through rain on the 17th of the second Hebrew month. Noah's ark and its eight passengers rested on the mountains of Ararat on the 17th of the seventh month (right in the middle of God's annual Holy period known as the Feast of Tabernacles).

Jesus Christ gained a complete victory over death and the grave when God resurrected him near sunset on Nisan 17 (Saturday, April 8, 30 A.D.).

In the book of 1Corinthians the thirteenth chapter, the seventeenth mention of the word 'love' comes when the apostle Paul states that it is the GREATEST gift of all (1Corinthians 13:13). God's unending love (John 3:16) is truly victorious over all things. Those who stay faithful to God to the end of their lives will gain the victory over the grave when they are miraculously brought back to life (see 1Corinthians 15).

Daniel 7's beasts have seven heads and ten horns, for a total number of 17. They represent world-ruling powers from Daniel's time to the Second Coming of Jesus. The devil's end-time system (Revelation 13) will have seven heads and ten horns, which totals 17. All mankind will very soon obey and worship the devil and the Beast power. They will war against those who have faith in Jesus and keep the commandments, thus achieving a victory (though short-lived) against God's people (Revelation 13:1 - 8).

True Christians, however, will gain the ultimate victory over God's adversaries when he resurrects them back to life (Revelation 15:2; 20:4). One of the major themes of the Day of Atonement (commonly referred to as <u>Yom Kippur</u>), which occurs in the seventh Hebrew month on the tenth day, is the binding of Satan (see Revelation 20). Thus, 10 plus 7 equal the number 17, which testifies to Christ's perfect overcoming of Satan. (Paragraphs taken from biblestudy.org)

In the year 2017 God is renewing His Covenant with you as He declared in Genesis 17:1-17, if you'll turn to Him wholeheartedly. Will you live your life on purpose and walk out the plans of God? If Abraham did not move when God told him to take a step, he would have never experienced the wealth. *"When Abram was ninety-nine years old, the Lord appeared to him and said, "I am God Almighty; walk before me faithfully and be blameless. Then I will make my covenant between me and you and will greatly increase your numbers." Abram fell facedown, and God said to him, "As for me, this is my covenant with you: You will be the father of many nations. No longer will you be called Abram; your name will be Abraham, for I have made you a father of many nations. I will make you very fruitful; I will make nations of you, and kings will come from you. I will establish my covenant as an everlasting covenant between me and you and your*

descendants after you for the generations to come, to
be your God and the God of your descendants after
you."

Abraham didn't understand his full
purpose until he took a step. Are you taking a
step? You're waiting and praying to God while
He's waiting on you to accept your call and take
the first step.

Appearances of the number seventeen

Rehoboam, son of Solomon and they first
king of Judah after the United Kingdom split in
930 B.C., reigned for 17 years (930 to 913 B.C.).

The book of James has material from
seventeen Old Testament books. The book of 1
Corinthians has 17 direct quotations from the Old
Testament.

One of the longest names found in the
word of God, containing 17 letters, is
Chushanrishathaim (Judges 3:8).

How does the number 17 symbolize
our standing with God?

In Romans 8:35 the apostle Paul asks a simple question which is "What shall separate us from the love of Christ?" (HBFV). He extends his question a little more by asking if the following seven things could separate us, which are tribulation, persecution, distress, nakedness, famine, the sword or any other danger. He then tells us ten things that CANNOT get between our God and us, which are life, death, principalities, powers, angels, things present or to come, depth, height or anything created. Thus, we have 7 + 10 = 17, representing a Christian's perfect and eternal standing with God through Christ. (biblestudy.org)

Additional Biblical Meaning of 17

Genesis 7:11-13 NIV "In the six hundredth year of Noah's life, on the seventeenth day of the second month---on that day all the springs of the great deep burst forth, and the floodgates of the heavens were opened. And rain fell on the earth forty days and forty nights. On that very day Noah and his sons, Shem, Ham and

Japheth, together with his wife and the wives of his three sons, entered the ark."

Genesis 8:4 NIV "and on the seventeenth day of the seventh month the ark came to rest on the mountains of Ararat."

Genesis 37:2 NIV "This is the account of Jacob's family line. Joseph, a young man of **seventeen**, was tending the flocks with his brothers, the sons of Bilhah and the sons of Zilpah, his father's wives, and he brought their father a bad report about them."

Judges 8:26 NIV "The weight of the gold rings he asked for came to **seventeen** hundred shekels, not counting the ornaments, the pendants and the purple garments worn by the kings of Midian or the chains that were on their camels' necks.

1 Kings 14:21 NIV "Rehoboam son of Solomon was king in Judah. He was forty-one years old when he became king, and he reigned **seventeen** years in Jerusalem, the city the Lord had chosen out of all the tribes of Israel in which to put his Name. His mother's name was Naamah; she was an Ammonite."

1 Kings 22:51 NIV "Ahaziah son of Ahab became king of Israel in Samaria in the **seventeenth** year of Jehoshaphat king of Judah, and he reigned over Israel two years."

2 Kings 13:1 NIV "In the twenty-third year of Joash son of Ahaziah king of Judah, Jehoahaz son of Jehu became king of Israel in Samaria, and he reigned **seventeen** years."

2 Kings 16:1 NIV "In the **seventeenth** year of Pekah son of Remaliah, Ahaz son of Jotham king of Judah began to reign."

1 Chronicles 24:15 NIV "the **seventeenth** to Hezir, the eighteenth to Happizzez"

1 Chronicles 25:24 NIV "the **seventeenth** to Joshbekashah, his sons and relatives"

1 Chronicles 26:30 NIV "From the Hebronites: Hashabiah and his relatives---**seventeen** hundred able men---were responsible in Israel west of the Jordan for all the work of the Lord and for the king's service."

2 Chronicles 12:13 NIV "King Rehoboam established himself firmly in

Jerusalem and continued as king. He was forty-one years old when he became king, and he reigned **seventeen** years in Jerusalem, the city the Lord had chosen out of all the tribes of Israel in which to put his Name. His mother's name was Naamah; she was an Ammonite."

Jeremiah 32:9 NIV "so I bought the field at Anathoth from my cousin Hanamel and weighed out for him **seventeen** shekels of silver."

According to (biblestudy.org), Psalm 83, verses 6 to 11, lists **seventeen** total enemies of Israel. Seven of these God destroyed in the past. The other ten foes will soon try to destroy the Israelites and "cut them off from being a nation." The Psalm, written by Davidic priests, beseeches the Eternal to treat Israel's future enemies like those in the past. The seven enemies God destroyed are the Midianites, Sisera, Jabin, Oreb, Zeeb, Zebah and Zalmunna. The future confederation prophesied to be against God's chosen are Edom, Ishmaelites, Moab, Hagarenes, Gebal, Ammon, Amalek, Philistines, Tyre and Assyria.

Seventeen is not only a prime or indivisible number, but it is also the seventh in the series of prime numbers (i.e., 1, 3, 5, 7, 11, 13, 17). The number **7** signifies **completeness**, which adds to the significance of the meaning of the number 17. Again, Bullinger explains (page 258): "In like manner *seventeen* being the seventh of the series, it partakes of and intensifies the significance of the number *seven*. Indeed, it is the combination or sum of the two perfect numbers—*seven* and *ten* - *seven* being the number of *spiritual* perfection, and *ten* of *ordinal* perfection. Contrasted together the significance of these two numbers is clear; and when united in the number seventeen we have a union of their respective meanings, *viz.*, spiritual perfection, plus ordinal perfection, or *the perfection of spiritual order*." Taken from www.kingdomandGlory.com

Chapter 4 – Victo-ries

On 9.1.16, God re-birth and re-launched, a new spiritual baby by the name of VICTORY! The blueprint of the baby's DNA is written in Psalm 91:1-16 NIV *"Whoever dwells in the shelter of the Most High will rest in the shadow of the Almighty." [2] I will say of the Lord, "He is my refuge and my fortress, my God, in whom I trust." [3] Surely, he will save you from the fowler's snare and from the deadly pestilence. [4] He will cover you with his feathers, and under his wings you will find refuge; his faithfulness will be your shield and rampart. [5] You will not fear the terror of night, nor the arrow that flies by day, [6] nor the pestilence that stalks in the darkness, nor the plague that destroys at midday. [7] A thousand may fall at your side, ten thousand at your right hand, but it will not come near you. [8] You will only observe with your eyes and see the punishment of the wicked. [9] If you say, "The Lord is my refuge," and you make the Most High your dwelling, [10] no harm will overtake you, no disaster will come near your tent. [11] For he will command his angels concerning you to guard you in all your ways; [12] they will lift you up in their hands, so that you will not strike your foot against a stone. [13] You will tread on the lion and the cobra; you will trample the great lion and the serpent. [14] "Because he loves me," says the Lord, "I will rescue him; I will protect him, for he acknowledges my name. [15] He will call on me, and I will answer him; I will be with him in trouble, I will deliver him and honor him. [16] With long life I will satisfy him and show him my salvation."*

You've been in His secret place, you've been incubated, He had angels watching over you, the storm did not overtake you, and **VICTORY** is here. You were waiting to participate in the birthing and re-birthing process and you've been tired and perhaps weary, but you've made it. God does everything in the spiritual realm first before the full manifestation on earth and in your life. You are about to see God's manifestations of victories in your life like you've never seen before.

God said the year 2017 is the year of many **Victo (ries).** It's the year of the **(RE's)** - Re-birth, Re-pentance, Re-aping a harvest, Re-plevin, Re-storation, Re-vival, Re-demption, Re-locate, Re-velations, Re-stitution, Re-newed - Re-lationships, Re-marry etc., etc., The year 5777/2017 will be a year of great Victories. In the Kingdom of God, you always fight and win from a place of VICTORY! In the book of Daniel, he had the VICTORY on the first day when he prayed, but because of the fight in the heavenlies, his answer was delayed for 21 days. I believe God delayed the answer so that Daniel could go through a process. So, it is for you, you already have the VICTORY, but it required a process. Abraham had the promise and the Victory, but it required a process (test) to get to the victory. Claim your VICTORY!

God gave me seven specific areas that you will experience His VICTORY and 57 RE-s that you can apply to your life.

The 7 specific areas for 2017 are:

1. Year of Manifestations, Victories and Promises being fulfilled
2. Year to walk in healing (Gen 20:17)
3. Year of the Triple Crown (Divine Perfection, Completion and Rest from Warfare
4. Year to live LiFE of Purpose
5. Year of the beginning of the 7 years of Abundance
6. Year to be Upgraded
7. Year of the switching of the Guards (From Elijah to Elisha's / Ruth to Naomi, Paul's to Timothy etc.)

57 Re's (Which ones will you activate?)

1. **RE-SET**
2. **RE-MNANTS Arise!**
3. **Re-st (from your enemies)**
4. Re-structure
5. Re-birth
6. RE-PENTANCE
7. **Re-plenish and multiply**
8. Re-flection
9. Re-alignment
10. Re-establish
11. Re-plevin
12. Re-compense
13. Re-stitution
14. Re-tribution
15. Re-location

16. Re-newal
17. **Re-vival**
18. Re-al Estate (time to own land)
19. Re-storation
20. Re-velation
21. Re-member the Lord (His Feasts)
22. Re-ap the Harvest
23. Re-volution
24. Re-formation
25. Re-deemed
26. Re-instate
27. Re-lease
28. Re-aquire
29. Re-activate
30. Re-dedicate
31. Re-levant
32. Re-spected
33. Re-adjust
34. Re-admission
35. Re-affirm
36. Re-align
37. Re-alms (new realms)
38. Re-ward
39. Re-marry
40. Re-assume your legal position
41. Re-assure
42. Re-attain
43. Re-awakening
44. Re-baptize
45. Re-ceive
46. Re-boot (time for an upgrade)
47. Re-build
48. Re-Strategize

49. Re-view (time to review the dreams and visions)
50. Re-process
51. Re-confirm
52. Re-commit
53. Re-claim your territory
54. Re-cliner (time to recline)
55. Re-lax (Be Still, God got this)
56. Re-ad, write and publish
57. **RE-ADY TO WALK IN YOUR PURPOSE, in your WEALTH!**

Sound of Victory

Psalm 118:15 NIV *"Shouts of joy and VICTORY resound in the tents of the righteous: "The Lord's right hand has done mighty things!"* In a recent word by Kim Potter, she says that the sound is the Sign of Abundance and she referred to 1 Kings 18:41-44 NIV **"And Elijah said to Ahab, "Go, eat and drink, for there is the sound of a heavy rain." So, Ahab went off to eat and drink, but Elijah climbed to the top of Carmel, bent down to the ground and put his face between his knees. "Go and look toward the sea," he told his servant. And he went up and looked. "There is nothing there," he said. Seven times Elijah said, "Go back." The seventh time the servant reported, "A cloud as small as a man's hand is rising from the sea." So, Elijah said, "Go and tell Ahab, 'Hitch up your chariot and go down before the rain stops you.'"**

Notice that it was the seventh time that the breakthrough came for Elijah. You may have felt like you've gone through the same situation repeatedly. Well this time it's the 7th time. The Year of Victory 5777/2017 is at hand. So, SHOUT!

Legal Authority

You had to go through the pain, trials, tribulations and sufferings. You had to experience the contractions and the birthing pains. It was designed by God to give you authority and influence in that area of your life. You can't have an anointing or authority in any area of life unless you've first walked through it. For you to be victorious in anything and to have legal authority you must first experience it, be tested in it so that you can have dominion over it.

To have wealth you must first know what it's like to be broke. To have authority in healing you must first be healed, which means that you had to be sick in some area of your life (financial, health, business etc.,). Jesus had to go through the test and trials and even death to win. He experienced temptation from the enemy. He experienced persecution. He paid the price and it was after the test, the spin cycle, that God granted Him the reward and gave Him the church as His bride. God had a strategy and so did Christ.

So, if you look at your life, the problems and heartaches that you have experienced and walked through, just know that it was God's way of granting you legal permission and authority over that area and now you can help someone else and build up the Kingdom of God. 2016 was your year to be broken, to experience transition, it was a year of reset, re-calibration, to go through the test, to experience His divine healing, to be challenged and now it's time to Celebrate because you have the VICTORY! *"Blessed (happy, to be envied) is the man who is patient under trial and stands up under temptation, for when he has stood the test and been approved, he will receive the victor's crown of life which God has promised to those who love Him."* James 1:12 AMP

Re-storation of broken Re-lationships

Broken relationships are one of the most overlooked area in life that we will start to see restoration and healing. One of the reasons why relational brokenness is not so apparent is because it's typical healing in the emotions which cannot be seen. The scars that are in the heart from emotional or verbal abuse cannot be seen with the naked eye, because they are internal. Sometimes we are not even aware that there's trauma until years later when what was buried surfaced and you thought you had dealt with it but perhaps you only buried it. Oftentimes most interpersonal relationship problems are derivatives from other problems from previous relationships. What tends to happen is this pattern of not dealing with problems becomes a learned behavior and the individual isn't even aware there's a problem because he or she operates in survival mode. Walk VICTORIOUSLY in your relationships and know that God is restoring that which was once broken.

Moments of Reflection..................

Pause and take a moment to reflect: Write down things that were lost or stolen that you would like returned.........

_____

_____

_____

_____

_____

_____

_____

_____

_____

_____

_____

_____

_____

_____

_____

_____

Chapter 5 – Resets & Remnants

God is saying that in this year of the Triple Crown, I am giving 3 Major Re-sets and each of them will come with almost three months of time for re-adjustment, re-alignment, re-boot, and re-structuring to get things in order. **What is a Reset?**

Just like a computer or smart phone, there comes a time when there needs to be an upgrade to the software or perhaps the equipment is not working well and needs fixing. So, it is now in our life. God is getting ready to upgrade those who have gone through the test and are ready for an upgrade. The new path where He's taking us, requires that we get our lives upgraded for the journey that's ahead.

God has a tremendous blessing for His people and He is such a patient and loving God that He is giving us time to get our lives in order. He is giving us time to get things together and to clean up our lives and prepare for the new upgraded life.

The First Major Reset was **October 3, 2016- Tishri 1, 5777 - Rosh Hashanah - Jewish Civil New Year**. This was a period that God allowed some to start getting their lives together. Personally, I was still within my sabbatical season with the Lord and it was during this time that God started giving me content and titles for the books that I would release. The first Reset last up until December 31, 2016.

The 2nd Major Reset - **January 1, 2017 -Gregorian New Year (Tevet 4, 5777)** goes all the way until **March 27, 2017**. This is the middle reset and the scripture that God used for this Reset is the exact middle of the bible and the shortest scripture in the bible with only two verses. It is Psalm 117 *"Praise the Lord, all you nations; extol him, all you peoples. For great is his love toward us, and the faithfulness of the Lord endures forever. Praise the Lord."*

If you look at the 2nd Reset, you will see a pattern and sequence of numbers that validates that God is truly speaking to His people. The 2nd reset, which is the middle reset, is found in the middle of the bible with only two verses. The reset began on 1/17 and the bible verse is the 117th Psalm. This is not a coincidence as there's no coincidence in God.

The 3rd Major Reset commence on **March 28, 2017 (Nisan 1, 5777)** - Jewish Biblical New Year. This is the time when the children of Israel were in preparation to depart from Egypt on their journey to the Promise Land. This reset period goes from March 28th – June 1st (a total of 66 days).

Effective June 2nd / Sivan 8 (new beginnings), it's time to walk in your divine purpose and align with God and the things that He is doing. This reset and new kingdom life is not for everyone, it's for the **REMNANTS** - the Kingdom Ambassadors. It's for those that are ready to live and walk out their divine purpose and live a Kingdom LiFE™.

The Remnants

There's a TRANSFER of Leadership at hand. A changing of the guards. We will see God raising up the Youth, the 20's, 30's and the 40's. The 50's, 60's and some 70's that have not gotten their opportunity to lead will now get that opportunity. He's raising up a new set of leaders and warriors to carry the baton as the race continues to the finish line.

God is doing some age reversals, renewals and resets and so the 42's will now feel and look like the 24-year-old and so on. There will be a change from the Moses' to the Joshua's. From the Elijah's to the Elisha's and from the Naomi's to the Ruth's. These new leaders are the Re-mnants. God is raising up a Joshua generation with the Key of David, with the Joseph's Anointing and the spirit of Deborah to fulfill all of God's prophetic promises to Israel and His

Beloved Church. While God is releasing the **FRESH VOICES** (*the Joshua's, Joseph's, Ester's, Deborah's to birth forth something new; He* still need the Paul's, Elisha's, Peter's and so on, to be mentors and guides as they pass the leadership baton.

Don't Hold on to the Baton

Sometimes those that have labored for years, can get envious when a new kid comes on the block. However, God is saying, oh I have not forgotten you. You're a part of my strategy and turn around. I'm using you like Elijah to build up the Elisha's and your reward is GREAT. I'm now using the Joshua's, Caleb's, Deborah's and Esther's, to lead in the promise land because they're strong. All will inherit and receive his or her reward.

Chapter 6 – Re-births

Over the course of 2016 and even now in 2017, God continues to show me and many others, His heavenly signs in the skies through His **RAINBOWS**. Some of the rainbows have been double rainbows with distinct colors. Some have been the full circular rainbows (which is what they really are) and even recently, my husband and I had the awesome privilege to see a triple rainbow. These have been signs and confirmations from the Lord re-minding us that His Promises must come to pass. Some of the rainbows have been so visible that my 6-year-old son said, *"he wishes he could slide down on the rainbow like a roller coaster."* God has been showing us signs and wonders to re-mind us that His Promises are YES & AMEN and it's time to step forth and live your life on Purpose.

Time to Step Forth

While being in the Secret Place with God, He directed me to Genesis 9:9-16 to confirm his re-birth of **Promise** and **Purpose**. Around 9:09pm on 9/9/16, God said that He's re-minding us of His promises that He made from the beginning. Genesis 9:9-16 NIV states *"I now establish my covenant with you and with your descendants after you...I establish my covenant with you: Never again will all life be destroyed by the waters of a flood; never again will there be a flood to destroy the earth." And God said, "This is the sign of the covenant I am making between me and you and every living creature with you, a covenant for all generations to come: I have set my* rainbow *in the clouds, and it will be the sign of the covenant between me and the earth. Whenever I bring clouds over the earth and the rainbow appears in the clouds, I will remember my covenant between me and you and all living creatures of every kind. Never again will the waters become a flood to destroy all life. Whenever the rainbow appears in the clouds, I will see it and remember the everlasting covenant between God and all living creatures of every kind on the earth."*

In the year of **VICTO-RIES**, God is saying to us, I have seen the rainbows in the cloud. I have seen your situations, but just as I made a promise to Noah, I am reminding you that I will fulfill My promises to you. Since we are descendants of Noah each time we see the **RAINBOW** in the sky let it be a reminder that God's promises are sure. What promises are you waiting to see manifest? I know many are awaiting the manifestation of the promises and prophetic words and it seems like Goliath is always standing in the way, but God says you will begin to see a season of MANIFESTATIONS come forth NOW!

There were also other re-births that took place between October – December 2016. On 10/10/16 – Heaven had a rebirth of, Kingdom, Love, and Supernatural. On 11/11/16 - the Church Rebirth Salvation, Five-Fold, and Royalty. On 12/12/16, Earth, re-birth Healing, Wealth, Awakenings and Revivals. These births already took place and so you can participate in any of these blessings NOW!

Fight for your Promises

While God's PROMISES are sure, the process is something He normally does not share. The process is based on the decisions and choices that you make. God promised me that I would be the mother of three and that one of the three would be a son. What He didn't tell me was that I would have to go through a fight to birth forth that son. My son was declared dead in my womb. I was hospitalized for weeks. One night, the resident doctor on duty decided that he was going to abort the baby because there was no life in my womb. It was a good thing that I was familiar with healthcare and knew that I could refuse care. I did that, because while I couldn't feel my son in my womb, I knew by faith that He was alive.

Today this son is seven years old. I had to go through a process to birth forth the promise. God used the process that I went through to help so many other families that had difficulty conceiving, going through losses or simply just giving birth to a dream or vision. Through this process, I published a book "Pregnant with a Promise" that is in high-demand. You will need to fight for your prophetic promises. Do not let the enemy win. You already have the VICTORY! Your process could end up being a book, TV Show, Ministry, Conference or a Testimony that's designed to be a blessing to you and to others. I decree and declare that your promises and purpose will not die, but will live.

Chapter 7 - Seven Steps to Breakthrough

Life is a Journey and a journey requires a process to get to the destination. God could have birth Christ as a full-grown man at the age of 33, but He didn't do that. God allowed Jesus to go through a process to birth forth the promise of re-demption. A person experiences the most pain and brokenness right before breakthrough. If you recall right before Jesus was getting ready to RE-DEEM us, to die for us, the pain and pressure intensified. In fact, he travailed and asked God to remove the cup from Him. He asked his buddies to pray for and with him, but they fell asleep.

I know at times you may feel alone. I decree and declare that God will release angels on your behalf right now to minister to you and to help you through this season and time. Jesus is the best example of the steps that are needed for breakthrough. In the book of Luke when Jesus was ministering to the multitudes there came a point when they all got hungry and needed to eat. The disciples told Jesus to send the people away so that they can go and eat and find a place to stay. Jesus in-turn would demonstrate the 7 steps to receive a breakthrough and showed how we all have authority for breakthrough if we follow these simple steps.

The text reads, Luke 9:10-17 NIV *"When the apostles returned, they reported to Jesus what they had done. Then he took them with him and they withdrew by themselves to a town called Bethsaida, but the crowds learned about it and followed him. He welcomed them and spoke to them about the kingdom of God, and healed those who needed healing. Crowds followed him and he spoke about the Kingdom of God and those that needed to be healed were healed. Late in the afternoon the Twelve came to him and said, "Send the crowd away so they can go to the surrounding villages and countryside and find food and lodging, because we are in a remote place here." He replied, "You give them something to eat." They answered, "We have only five loaves of bread and two fish---unless we go and buy food for all this crowd." (About five thousand men were there.) But he said to his disciples, "Have them sit down in groups of about fifty each." The disciples did so, and everyone sat down. Taking the five loaves and the two fish and looking up to heaven, he gave thanks and broke them. Then he gave them to the disciples to distribute to the people. They all ate and were satisfied, and the disciples picked up twelve basketfuls of broken pieces that were left over.*

In Luke 9: 11-17

The Steps are:

1.   SPOKE (Decree & Declaration) Luke 9:13 NIV He replied, *"You give them something to eat." They answered, "We have only five loaves of bread and two fish---unless we go and buy food for all this crowd."* (Use what you have)

2.   STRATEGY - Luke 9:14 NIV (About five thousand men were there.) But he said to his disciples, *"Have them sit down in groups of about fifty each."*

It's time to get a STRATEGY because it's BREAKTHROUGH time. Having a Strategy is so critical. Can you imagine the chaos it would have been if Jesus did not have a Strategy? If the multitudes were not sitting in groups of 50, it would be disastrous to feed everyone without them bombarding Jesus and the disciples.

3.   ACTIVATION - Luke 9:16 NIV *Taking the five loaves and the two fish* (7 Tools) 7 WORDS, 7 years of blessings, 7 streams of income, 7 mountains come down. 5000 People!

4.   APPEAL TO HEAVEN Luke <u>9:16</u> *and looking up to heaven...* (John Henderson has a great book on this)

5.   GAVE THANKS Luke <u>9:16</u>

6.   BROKE THEM (5776/2016) Luke <u>9:16</u> (must be broken before you experience a breakthrough) spirit of Multiplication (COMMUNION) - Unity in GOD!

Some of you are in Step 6 right now, waiting and ready to eat with LEFTOVERS. You've been broken, felt somewhat hopeless, can feel the wind of change coming, anticipating the great and mighty move of God, BUT WONDERING WHEN WILL IT HAPPEN.

Some of you are in the broken stages right now and we're about to EAT and eat good with leftovers - 12 basketful.

THEY ALL ATE / Luke <u>9:17</u> God says 5777/2017 starts the 7 years of blessings and abundance. It's time to eat. During Joseph's 7 years of abundance, what did they do? They all had something to eat, right? Joseph had a plan, God gave him the solution to the problem. He gave him a Strategy. Joseph was a Strategist which made him a Solutionist all because he walked in his purpose.

Activate your BREAKTHROUGH

Right before a baby is born as its coming through the birth canal it's not getting any air. You may feel like you're drowning, like you can't breathe but God wants you to know that in a quick second suddenly, your head has made it through. You're coming out. Time to cut the umbilical cord and eat. Put your Strategy in place.

As an Executive Vice President for a Firm, I go into organizations, churches etc., and review, implement or coach them through their strategic plans. It's my #1 selling product and service in my business. It's a strategic plan that companies like Starbucks, Apple and others use to get them from a thousandaire company to millionaire, to billionaire and now heading to trillionaire. There are churches today that have a great vision and awaiting the promises of God but do not have a Strategy. The members in the church do not know the Strategy. There are families with no Strategy and no sense of direction.

In a story in Luke 16, Jesus was giving an example of a man that used wisdom and implemented a strategy. This (manager) employee was messing up and about to lose his job. When he realized it, he started to think of a Strategy that will change the situation. He figured out a plan and it went well. What's surprising though is what Jesus said. He said that those in the world are wiser and take care of their own versus Christians.

Christian's seem to be the only organized group of people that don't seem to work together to build up the kingdom of God. Why? Because there's no Strategy in place. Most Christians seem to be okay with the status quo of life, but GOD SEES STATUS QUO AS LUKEWARM and HE SPREWS THOSE OUT. YOU DON'T WANT TO BE the worker bee that is happy with just getting a paycheck, and able to afford you cellular phone bill and catch a movie, and consider life to be good. That's not Kingdom living. What happened to being the head and not the tail? What about running the business and not working for others? What about owning the credit unions and the bank? What about living that royal kingdom life?

*According to Luke 16:1-8,10 NIV "**Jesus told his disciples: "There was a rich man whose*** *manager was accused of wasting his possessions. So, he called him in and asked him, 'What is this I hear about you? Give an account of your management, because you cannot be manager any longer.' "The manager said to himself, 'What shall I do now? My master is taking away my job. I'm not strong enough to dig, and I'm ashamed to beg--- I know what I'll do so that, when I lose my job here, people will welcome me into their houses.' "So, he called in each one of his master's debtors. He asked the first, 'How much do you owe my master?' "Nine hundred gallons of olive oil,' he replied. "The manager told him, 'Take your bill, sit down quickly, and make it four hundred and fifty.' "Then he asked the second, 'And how much do you owe?' "'A thousand bushels of wheat,' he replied. "He told him, 'Take your bill and make it eight hundred.' "The master commended the dishonest manager because he had acted shrewdly. For the people of this world are more shrewd in dealing with their own kind than are the people of the light. And the lord commended the unjust steward, because he had done wisely: for the children of this world are in their generation wiser than the children of light."*

The text summarizes the matter. Get a STRATEGY. One can be found here http://www.carolynganderson.com/coaching.*html*. *The* law of promotion is only activated when you have a strategy and when God can trust you with the little that you have, then He will give you the plenty and enlarge your coast.

So, while some of you are in still in STEP 6- right now and you're ready to EAT good with leftovers - 12 basketfuls, God want you to take some time and begin to implement, review or revise your strategy and make things happen. The year 2016 has been so difficult that many begin to question what's their significance in life because of what they went through. You have a new beginning.

Anointed for Kingdom Building

In 2 Samuel, Chapter 6 it talks about the story of David when he was bringing the Ark of the Covenant back to Jerusalem. David's purpose was to place the ark of the covenant on his shoulders but instead David placed it on a cart and was in the background behind those who are leading the cart. One of David's servant Uzzah, reached out and grabbed the Ark of the Covenant as it was falling in reverence and respect to God. God struck Uzzah dead, because while he was doing a great deed, it wasn't his purpose to first be carrying the Ark of the Covenant and second to touch it. David was angry and perplexed and he left the Ark of the Covenant at the house of Obed-Edom the Gittite.

After three months David went and brought the Ark of the Covenant to his house and he did it the right way. David went ahead of all the men, unlike before he was in the background. David's purpose was to be in front, to be the leader and the one anointed to carry the Ark of the Covenant. Noah's purpose at the time was to build an ARK. I can only imagine that many were laughing at Noah. He was not just building a boat, but an ARK. Perhaps God's purpose for you is to build or re-build something and it may seem laughable. One of the things I have learned is that if the vision is easy enough for me to accomplish it then it's not BIG enough for God.

The Lord anointed David to re-turn the Ark of the Covenant to the city of David. It was his Purpose and he needed to walk it out. I've been there, where I was in the background and God was telling me something to do, but instead I would ask my husband to do it or I would share it with others who I believed at the time were more qualified than I was. No one else can walk out your purpose and no one else is anointed to do what God has told you to do.

It's time to re-calibrate, re-set, re-shuffle some things around, re-route, re-strategize, because your Purpose must shine. It's time to take your rightful place in the KINGDOM, because these next 7 years, you will need to be in position for the Kingdom Mandate. Which mountain/s are you called to? You will be the lender and not the borrower. It's time to own credit unions, be the CFO, the President or Prime Minister, be the Queen or the King, a supreme court judge, own that business, lead the ministry. You are the head and not the tail. It's time to live in the PALACE and re-ign. Your life is about to be invaded with VICTORIES. The time is NOW says the Lord!

Prayer: Pray for God to re-veal to you His PURPOSE for your life, if you don't already know what it is.

Activation: Review any prophetic words that you have received. Go back through them because God says He's going to re-veal some things that you missed before. It's time for MANIFESTATIONS.

Chapter 8 - Palace Time

Seasons exist within cycles and cycles exist within TIME. Seasons are cycles or cyclical but TIME is Constant and Dimensional. For example, when Joseph went to live in the Palace it was his time to rule and reign. Yet his time would be broken down into 7-year cycles, which were the **Seven years of Abundance** and 7 years of drought. Within those seven years, each year had 4 different seasons and each season, had months, weeks, days, hours and seconds. However, no matter what season or cycle Joseph was going through, once he entered the **PALACE** to live out his true purpose, he remained there for the rest of his life. I am decreeing that when you enter your Palace Season that you will not go back.

Around August 2016, God sent a specific and clear word to me and said that 5777/2017 will be the beginning of the seven years of abundance and wealth as it was in the days of Joseph. He said that many have been in the pit season, Potiphar's house season, prison season and now it's time for promotion to the Palace Season.

It's a time for Elevation, Replevin and Wealth. It's time for you to use the gifts and talents that God gave you to take your rightful place in the Kingdom of God. It's time for you to use your delegated authority and be on the command post. Like Joseph your Palace time is coming. In my book from the **Pit to the Palace**, I share that all life's experiences that we go through is to get us tough enough and equipped to lead like Joseph and to see the manifestations of God's promises. God always have an appointed time for everything and no man or devil can stop it. God's set and appointed time to live the Kingdom life and enter the PALACE is at hand.

It is in the **PALACE** that Joseph would live for the rest of his life and this is where the 7-year cycle within TIME began. Joseph had 7 good years and the 7 not so good years, but he was never without and the people came to him for their supply of food. So, shall it be for us. What will be your wealth strategy for the next 7 years? Promotion comes now because effective 5777 / 2017 it begins the 7 years of ABUNDANCE and BLESSINGS as you prepare and store up grain (Sustenance) for the next 7 years.

There's coming a time where the world will turn to the church for provision. The transfer of wealth is here, but you must be prepared. The triple **CROWN** is at hand as God is carefully and uniquely orchestrating his divine timing and will for your life. The Year 2017 and 5777 is a significant marker in TIME. We will experience the joy and glory that comes when Heaven, Earth and the Church are in divine alignment and working in partnership. God is getting ready to show forth his SUPERNATURAL powers and to show the world that He is God! It's time for Divine Alignment.

On October 10, 2016, (Tishri 8, 5777) on the Jewish calendar, by day they were 2 numbers apart (10-8) and on November 11, 2016 (Cheshvan 10) the dates were one number difference. And oh, December 1, 2016 was also the 1st day of the month Kislev on the Jewish Calendar. For the first time in a long time the Jewish calendar and the Gregorian Calendar were in divine alignment.

Before the foundations of the world, God knew that alignment would come. He knew that you would be alive at this present moment to see His divine timetable playing out. Walk in your year of VICTO-RIES and experience God's Grace for completion, perfection and divine rest AND WEALTH being transferred to you.

Chapter 9 - Wealth Transfer

Since the time of Exodus from EGYPT, there has not been a major transfer of Wealth for God's People. This also means that since the time when Christ was on earth and ascended there hasn't been a major WEALTH TRANSFER either. I believe that the time is NOW. According to Exodus 3:20-22 NIV it states *"So I will stretch out my hand and strike the Egyptians with all the wonders that I will perform among them. After that, he will let you go. "And I will make the Egyptians favorably disposed toward this people, so that when you leave you will not go empty-handed. Every woman is to ask her neighbor and any woman living in her house for articles of silver and gold and for clothing, which you will put on your sons and daughters. And so, you will plunder the Egyptians."*

This major Wealth Transfer requires a process just like it was in the days of the Exodus. God said His first step in the WEALTH transfer and major VICTORIES that the year 5777 and 2017 brings will be MASS HEALING. It's time for the unhealthy life to EXODUS. It's time for it to go! You can be healed in your mind and body, finance, faith and relationships. When the children of Israel were getting ready to leave their past and cross over into their PROMISED LAND, there was none sick or diseased amongst them.

There was no death in their midst, because the blood of Jesus had passed over them. At the time of their Exodus, they were all healthy because they needed the strength for the Journey. So, shall it be in the Kingdom of God, it's one thing to acquire finance and be financially stabled but with serious health problems. God said He needs you to be healthy and strong so that you can CREATE and receive WEALTH, therefore be Healed in Jesus Name. According to Psalm 105:37-45 NIV *"He brought out Israel, laden with silver and gold, and from among their tribes no one faltered. Egypt was glad when they left, because dread of Israel had fallen on them. He spread out a cloud as a covering, and a fire to give light at night. They asked, and he brought them quail; he fed them well with the bread of heaven. He opened the rock, and water gushed out; it flowed like a river in the desert. For he remembered his holy promise given to his servant Abraham. He brought out his people with rejoicing, his chosen ones with shouts of joy; he gave them the lands of the nations, and they fell heir to what others had toiled for---that they might keep his precepts and observe his laws. Praise the Lord."* Be healed!

WEALTH was transferred to Joseph because he went through the **process** of healing that led to him walking out his PURPOSE. Purpose is a journey and not a destination. Joseph went from being chosen and the most favored son to slavery, accusation, prison to being in the Palace. Many of you may feel like you're in a prison season or you may literally be in Jail or in Prison and you feel a calling on your life and a tugging for your Purpose to truly be established. God is saying that as you prepare yourself in the prison season, where your GIFT makes room for you, in no time you shall reap what you have sown. In Acts 12:12-16 NIV, while the people were praying for Peter to be released from Prison, an Angel of the Lord released Peter and he went and knocked at the door to announce his release. God is releasing you from your pain, suffering, prison season and from debt because you've knocked at the door and it's time for it to be OPENED.

The major transfer will take place when you STEP into your PURPOSE. What were you created to be? Just like anything in life there's a process to get to the result. Moses had to go through a process to redeem the children of Israel. David had to walk through a process to rule in the palace. I had to go through a process to get to where I am today and so shall you. Every process has STEPS and here's an example of the Wealth Transfer process that was outlined in Exodus.

Steps of Wealth Transfer

In Exodus, there were steps that were taken for the major **WEALTH TRANSFER.** While there are variations within a process may differ. Your process may be slightly different from mine, what remains the same is that you can't skip a step in the process, because that will be detrimental. The steps in Exodus are:

1. **Health/Healing** - There were no sick or diseased amongst the children of God. None died that followed the instructions and placed the blood on the doorposts. God said He needs you to be healthy and strong so that you can CREATE and receive WEALTH, so be Healed in Jesus Name. It's one thing to acquire finance and be financially stabled but with serious health problems. Be prepared for the Transfer of Wealth. Many are working hard now and they are doing it for you. *Psalm 105:44,* ***"He gave them the lands of the nations, and they fell heir to what others had toiled for..."*** Walk in your healing so that you can be prepared to step in your Finances that are ahead of you.

According to Genesis 20:17 AMP, *"So Abraham prayed to God, and God healed Abimelech and his wife and his female slaves, and they bore children,"* and the NIV version says, *"Then Abraham prayed to God, and God healed Abimelek, his wife and his female slaves so they could have children again."* So, the very first healing ever in the history of mankind was performed by God himself through the prayer of Abraham. Healing is VICTORY to anyone and Abimelek and his wife experienced complete victory after being healed.

It is no coincidence that the first appearance of healing is found exactly in the **20th Chapter and the 17th** verse of Genesis **(The Year 2017-Genesis 20:17).** With God, there's no coincidence. He is a God of timing and He is always on time. Beginning at Genesis 1 - God orchestrated and created everything in His specific time. He is the God of perfect timing. We find His perfect timing all throughout the Bible. God rested on the 7th day, Christ rose on the 3rd day, Noah and his family were saved (8 of them). The Father continues to reveal Himself to us through times and seasons, numbers, dates, signs and wonders. It's TIME for you to living a healthy life. 2017 is your YEAR!

2. **Finance** - Resources (Money in the form of jewelry, gold and silver) were given to the children of Israel. The Egyptians gave many of their prized possessions to the children of God as they were getting ready for their Exodus from Egypt to the Promise Land. So, shall it be for you. Many will give to you.

3. **Faith** - they came to a point where they saw no way out. In front of them was the Red Sea (Ocean, Major Lake) and the Egyptian army was chasing them down. By Faith Moses raised his staff and parted the Red Sea. The people had faith as they crossed the Red Sea.

4. **Relationship** - they needed each other and they needed to re-establish a relationship and a covenant with God. Relationships will be so strategic during this time of TRANSFER.

5. **Purpose** – know what your role and purpose is and position yourself to walk in the fullness of your purpose. If you are

not sure about your purpose, I have a purpose finder course online that you can take:

http://transform.carolynganderson.com/

6. **Strategy** – get a strategy for your life. God is a God of Strategy. He knew how and when He needed to create everything. You will need to make sure you have the right vision, people, and tools in your toolbox to not just obtain the Wealth, but to grow it and keep it. When Joseph interpreted the dream of the Pharaoh, he took it a little further and shared the Strategy with him. It was the Strategy that allowed Joseph to be promoted to a position of power and influence. You can find a Strategy here: http://www.carolynganderson.com/coaching.html

Get ready! You are about to experience a major Wealth Transfer if you have been in position and prepared for it. Get ready for the overnight promotions from the Prison season to the Palace season.

Chapter 10 – The Awakening Strategy

For the last year, I have been hearing stories of revivals and awakenings and a great big change that's coming. My husband and I are very familiar with awakenings as we've been ministering about the awakening for the last 4 years. Around Rosh Hashanah 5776 (September 2015) and especially starting in March 2016, I became intentional about listening and reading what other Prophets were saying, as I knew God was up to something BIG. He was using them as confirmations for what He was telling me in secret. At that time, I needed to subject myself to other Prophets as God was giving each of them parts for the whole. According to 1 Corinthians 13:9 NIV it states that *"For we know in part and we prophesy in part..."* therefore it was imperative that I participated and came into agreement with the Prophets during that timeframe.

Now, it's God's set time for me to release the part for the body of Christ that He has given me. We are to subject ourselves one to another especially since no one person has all the answers but only our part that God has given us. I'm humbled to have a piece of God's Great and mighty plan that's at hand.

God has released an awakening strategy that you can participate in. He has already qualified and equipped you to pursue your rightful position in the Kingdom. According to Colossians 1:2 AMP *"Giving thanks to the Father, Who has qualified and made us fit to share the portion which is the inheritance of the saints (God's holy people) in the Light."* Therefore, the time is now for you to activate where you fit in and what you have been gifted to carry out.

The STRATEGY

✓ **Apostles** - planting and building up the leaders (pastors), churches etc.

✓ **Prophets** - laying the foundation and bringing a prophetic word to the people. They are to travel and prophesy what thus says the Lord.

✓ **Evangelist** - spreading the word of God on the highways and byways, going into homes and ministering the word of God. Stirring up the spirit of God in the people.

✓ **Pastors** - ministering to the people, being a shepherd over the sheep. Pastor of different groups to those assigned to them.

- ✓ **Teachers** - rightly dividing the word. Teaching the Word of God for understanding and revelation.

- ✓ **Revivals** – hosting revivals for the saints (can't revive something that was never birth) focus on reviving the Christians or the backsliders.

- ✓ **Missionaries** - going on a mission to help the sick, poor and the homeless and visiting those in hospitals. Helping the orphans, widows and those less fortunate. Missionaries are not to be in the four walls preaching. This is where they come to be re-fueled. A Missionary is a full-time work and so you should have systems set up in place that provides financial support as you go on the journey.

- ✓ **Intercessors and Prayer Warriors-** praying strategic prayers, while we pray for each other.

- ✓ **Gifts** - Each Christian using their gift in the KINGDOM (whether marketplace or in the physical church)

- ✓ **Adopt a Block** -**Transform a City** going into the neighborhoods to clean (one block at a time) build trust, show and tell (show God and then tell Christ). Provide basic human needs first and then share the good news.

✓ **Chaplains** - Police Chaplains, Disaster Chaplains, Sex & Human Trafficking etc. Marketplace Chaplains working full time in Corporate firms.

✓ **Safe Havens/Group Homes** - homes for the poor, widow, abused, lost, homeless, broken. Christian's purchasing the homes and turning them into shelters.

✓ **Workplace Chaplains** - getting into the workplace and becoming a part of the leadership teams.

7 MOUNTAIN STRATEGY

1. **Businesses** - supporting Christian led businesses. Starting your own business. Becoming the next CEO, Leader, Executive etc. **Only** use your money to purchase and support companies that you believe in and has the same values as you do.

2. **Entertainment** - Christian Entertainment, Songs and Music for the Now Generation that edifies GOD. Talk Shows, Public Figure that represents Christ.

3. **Family** – restoring Kingdom Families, Getting the fathers back into the homes, Marriages between one man and one woman, protecting the entity of family, and standing for justice.

4. **Government** - praying for the leaders. Become a government official, politician yourself so that you can be the decision maker and perhaps the next president of the nation where you reside. Laws that protect families and matters important to Christians. Getting into the systems and becoming the next government officials.

5. **Education** – building our own Kingdom Schools, where the children and taught biblical history and learn who they are at an early age. We need prayer back into the schools and for someone to take the mantle and fight to get back prayers in the school. We need real Kingdom Universities and Colleges, that are teaching economic principles from a biblical perspective.

6. **Religion/Ministry** – it's time to break down the boundaries and barriers of religion that have left many people bound. Man-made rules and regulations have taken the place of sound biblical teaching and have pushed many away from the church. It's time to bring the prodigals back and teach and show them true love, because God is love. Churches will not look the way that it always has, as there's a new way to have church that's being birth right now.

7. **Media** – Time to share the GOOD NEWS! It is time for us to not implode our homes with all the negativity that's happening in and around the world, but to have more Christian news stations, sharing and shedding the good that's happening in the world. We can do this!

These are just some examples of ways that you can occupy your space and walk out your purpose in life. I am sure that whatever your purpose is in life that it fits within one of those spheres above. Therefore, activate your occupation and allow your gift to make financial room for you.

Summary

As you prepare to decree and declare these 77 scriptures over your life, there's a very important step that is the pre-requisite before your declarations. To receive these benefits, you must first be a son or daughter of the Highest. One of the gifts of being a child of God is that you get complete access all His Benefits.

According to Psalm 103:2-14,17-19,22 NIV *"Praise the Lord, my soul, and forget not all his benefits--- who forgives all your sins and heals all your diseases, who redeems your life from the pit and crowns you with love and compassion, who satisfies your desires with good things so that your youth is renewed like the eagle's. The Lord works righteousness and justice for all the oppressed. He made known his ways to Moses, his deeds to the people of Israel: The Lord is compassionate and gracious, slow to anger, abounding in love. He will not always accuse, nor will he harbor his anger forever; he does not treat us as our sins deserve or repay us according to our iniquities. For as high as the heavens are above the earth, so great is his love for those who fear him as far as the east is from the west, so far has he removed our transgressions from us. As a father has compassion on his children, so the Lord has compassion on those who fear him; for he knows how we are formed, he remembers that we are dust. But from everlasting to everlasting the*

Lord's love is with those who fear him, and his righteousness with their children's children---with those who keep his covenant and remember to obey his precepts. The Lord has established his throne in heaven, and his kingdom rules over all. Praise the Lord, all his works everywhere in his dominion. Praise the Lord, my soul." When you belong to God you have access to all these benefits and more. One of His great blessing is healing.

Years ago, my father had prostate cancer and he underwent surgery to remove the cancer. For about two years everything was fine and it appeared that my dad was cured or in remission as some call in. Tragically the cancer came back or came back from hiding and this time it was more potent and powerful than the first time. His doctors pretty much said that there was nothing else they can do for him. He was just told to get regular checkups and hope that something changed. Thus, his disease became a death sentence waiting and hoping for a healing miracle.

My husband and I are both Pastors and one Sunday after I ministered and gave an open invitation for an altar call, to my surprise my dad came to the altar. Growing up, I never saw my dad attend church, but he always made sure that we went to church. The only time I saw him at a church service was at a funeral and I don't recall him being inside the church. He mostly hung outside. We grew up in Jamaica and it was mostly over 80 degrees so being outside was never a problem for him or anyone that wanted to be outside.

This Sunday something happened. I believed my dad was the last person that I prayed for. Prior to praying for him, I asked my dad if he was saved. I asked him if he had ever received Jesus Christ as his personal Lord and Savior. He had not, so then I asked him if he would like to be saved? Without hesitation, he said yes. After my father accepted Jesus Christ as his savior, I did something I have never done before. I looked directly at my father and said, "it is illegal for two spirits to dwell in the same body, therefore I command the spirit of cancer to leave his body now, because the Holy Spirit now lives there."

The following day was one of my dad's regular checkups for the cancer levels in his body. Long story short, to their amazing surprise there was **no cancer**. To this day, my dad is healed from cancer and enjoying his life playing golf and traveling. My point is when the earthly doctors have reached a point when they can do nothing else for you and if you're a child of God, that's when you turn to the Heavenly Doctor who can do the impossible. Become His child!

There's nothing too hard for God and when you have accepted His Son it gives you direct access to receive all the benefits from Him. It's no different from the places of employment how they each come with standard benefits such as health insurance. So, it is when you are in Christ Jesus, there are standard benefits that comes with being a part of the kingdom and one of those is healing. I should also point out that my dad also took the necessary steps thereafter and started to live a healthier life by eating the proper nutrition and exercising regularly. Being healed doesn't mean that you will not have to maintain a healthy lifestyle, because you will. You must take care of the temple, the finances, the relationships, and the mind that God has given you. Faith and works always work together. So, you must not only believe, but you must also pursue action steps to live a life of wholeness. Are you ready to live a life of complete dominion?

Confession

It's a simple process that takes less than 5 minutes. It's a three-step process as easy as ABC!

1. Accept Jesus Christ as your Lord and Savior
2. Believe in your heart that He died for you and that He is the risen savior that will return
3. Confess your sins and ask him to forgive you and forgive others as well

Congratulations! If you have just accepted Jesus Christ as your personal Lord & Savior, you can now fully participate in the blessings that are in store for you.

Date of Salvation: _____

77 Decrees & Declarations

This is the day that the Lord has made, we shall rejoice and be glad in it. Every good and perfect gift comes from God—therefore this year is both good and perfect because it comes from God!

2017 is a year of VICTORIES (the Re's), MANIFESTATIONS, PURPOSES established, HEALING, and WEALTH TRANSFER. It is a year when promises will be fulfilled, a year of abundance and OPEN DOORS, a year when many souls will be brought to the Kingdom of God

A year of signs, miracles and wonders, a year of prosperity for the righteous ones, a year when God's people shall rule and reign and inherit the earth, by being owners and lenders, and never borrowers. A YEAR OF BEING DEBT FREE and DRAMA FREE! BELIEVE IT & RECEIVE IT!

I decree and declare that:
1. This year 2017 will birth forth MANIFESTATIONS, VICTORIES, PURPOSES & PROMISES (MVP) being established in this YEAR of the LORD. We shall know our identity
2. This year of our lives will bring divine opportunities that WE will take full advantage of

3. This year is filled with wonderful surprises, supernatural breakthroughs, and miracles from Heaven
4. Today marks the end of a SAD (Standard Adult Day), depressing, discouraging past and the beginning of a prosperous, debt-free, disease-free, depression-free, happy future
5. God will grant us strategies for a prosperous and successful life
6. This year our Prayers will be answered SUDDENLY
7. We will Dance, Shout and Sing to the King
8. We will give more, because we HAVE MORE
9. Our minds will be filled with the knowledge of God's identity
10. We are empowered to accomplish that which we were born to do
11. We will become all that we were born to be
12. Every day of our lives is in sync with the perfect will of God
13. Our vision is clear
14. Our intentions are pure
15. His WILL BE DONE ON EARTH AS IT IS IN HEAVEN
16. Our relationships are healthy
17. Our minds are healthy
18. Our Finances Are Healthy
19. Our Faith is Healthy
20. Our God supplies all our needs according to His riches in glory

21. We live in a prosperous and healthy environment and we have GREAT NEIGHBORS
22. God has affirmed who we are
23. We are the light of the world and so we shall SHINE

I decree and declare that:

24. Joy, peace, prosperity, and success belongs to us
25. We have healthy friendships and are connected to the right people
26. We are filled with Love for God and for each other
27. We have healthy family members
28. We shall use our gifts and they will make room for us
29. We have found FAVOR with God and with man
30. We walk in divine delegated authority and we are the head and not the tail
31. We are world changers and Kingdom Builders
32. We will live a legacy and leave a legacy
33. We have an inheritance from our Heavenly Father and we will leave an inheritance for our future generations.
34. We are renewed and revived
35. We walk in greatness and our brilliance radiates daily
36. We will GLORIFY the GREAT KING
37. We are creative beings and we will live a creative life
38. We are millionaires

39. We are Royalty and unique

I decree and declare that:
40. Our minds are healthy and strong
41. We have a CLEAR VISION of our Future
42. We have the Wisdom of Solomon to make wise choices
43. We will pursue and recover all
44. Restoration belongs to us
45. The blessings of the Lord are upon us and we are rich
46. WE are healthy in our minds, body, soul and spirit
47. We are VICTORIOUS
48. We will no longer STRUGGLE, but will THRIVE
49. OUR enemies are subdued
50. WE ARE fruitful in all OUR endeavors
51. WE have 7 streams of income
52. We are the head and not the tail
53. We walk in abundance and we have dominion over earth's economic system
54. We are DEBT FREE and are not slaves to anyone
55. Wealth is transferred into OUR hands, NOW, BELIEVE IT AND RECEIVE IT
56. OUR income will always be greater than OUR expenses
57. Christ already paid the PRICE and by HIS STRIPES WE ARE HEALED
58. WE HAVE AN ABUNDANCE OF

money that WE need for day-to-day expenses

59. WE always have more than enough to give
60. WE will sow great seeds and we will reap even better seeds
61. WE joyfully give a tenth of all our earnings to God
62. There is no lack in our house, business or relationships
63. We finance God's people. The homeless, widow, orphans and the less fortunate are taken care of by us
64. OUR bank accounts are filled
65. OUR network and net worth increase daily
66. WE WILL SOW INTO THE LIVES OF PEOPLE THAT WILL ALLOW US TO REAP A HARVEST

I decree and declare that:

67. WE are resourceful
68. Everything THAT WE need is available to US when needed
69. The DOORS ARE WIDE OPEN and no man can close it
70. WE will only speak and share the GOOD NEWS
71. WE will praise God in and out of season
72. OUR NEXT 7 YEARS ARE FILLED WITH ABUNDANCE

73. WE are transformed daily by renewing our minds
74. WE walk in the Supernatural and God's presence is always with us
75. Our SOUL is well
76. WE are loved and will show LOVE
77. This year we will see MANIFESTATIONS, many VICTORIES and walk in our divine PURPOSE and see God's Promises being fulfilled in and through us.

YOUR PERSONAL PRAYER
(Pray Out Loud)

Our Father which art in Heaven, Hallowed, Mighty, Great and Powerful is your name. Let your Kingdom come and let your will be done in my life. Thank you for my daily bread… (the word). Forgive me for all my sins and debts as I forgive those that have sinned against me. Help me when I am tempted and save me from the evil one. For thine is the Kingdom the Power and the Glory, forever in Jesus Name!

Complete your personal prayer that's specific to you.

Dear God:

_____

_____

_____

_____

_____

_____

_____

Conclusion

"When he had received the drink, Jesus said, "It is finished." With that, he bowed his head and gave up his spirit" John 19:30 NIV

Three (3) of the most powerful words that seals the deal in any area of life, are "It is FINISHED." When Jesus spoke that out of His mouth, He meant it. You are already pre-destined to finish what God placed in you. You were destined for greatness before the foundations of the world. It's not by coincidence why you are reading this book, it's by divine appointment.

It is time for you to truly walk out your **PURPOSE** and to live a life with meaning. You are alive for such a time as THIS! You can no longer run from your true authentic you. Proverbs 19:21 AMP remind us that *"Many plans are in a man's mind, but it is the Lord's purpose for him that will stand"* and Romans 8:28 AMP *"We are assured and know that God being a partner in their labor all things work together and are fitting into a plan for good to and for those who love God and are called according to His design and purpose."* You are called according to HIS **PURPOSE**, so declare it and walk in it! YOUR TIME IS NOW!

Appreciation

First, I thank God for giving me life, health and strength and the many gifts to be who I am today. I thank Him for His son Jesus Christ, my savior and to the Holy Spirit for being my guide. Thanks to the most wonderful man on Earth - my husband Kevel A. Anderson, Sr., who loves me with all his heart and gives me the space and time that I need to live out my purpose in life. To our beautiful daughters, Christina and Chassidy and our son A.J. and nephew (like a son), C.J. for their love, laughter and support. To my mom, Sharon and a host of family and friends, thank you! Thanks to my publishing team and anyone who had anything to do with this book being released. Thank you for purchasing this book. Thank you!

About the Author

CAROLYN G. ANDERSON is the FRESH, dynamic and inspirational VOICE that's creating a buzz locally, nationally and internationally. She's a TV personality, Wealth Coach, Professor and the author of several books such as LiFE on Purpose, Transformational Leader-SHIP, Heal-thy LiFE, Focus & Get Results, Pregnant with a Promise, From the PIT to the PALACE and many more.

One of the nation's leading expert on the art of transformation, she is the Founder and Executive Vice President of Integrity Consulting and Coaching Enterprise (ICE), a corporate coaching, speaking and consulting firm with over 30 years of combined experience in strategic leadership, lean processes, six sigma, visioning, process improvement, coaching, contracting and negotiations, amongst other services.

A trained Army Soldier, Carolyn knows the discipline and FOCUS needed to hit the TARGET! She utilizes the same skills taught in the military to fight and WIN. She is a trusted voice and a ground-breaking Speaker-preneur. Amongst her many accomplishments and accolades, her all-time favorite role is being a mom and wife. Being a parent is a gift from God. She is purpose driven and lives life fully every day always walking in her divine calling.

She's an ordained Prophet and a Senior Leader of Kingdom LiFE Center, a global ministry. Learn more about her at www.carolynganderson.com or text DrCarolyn to 22828 to connect with her.

Be sure to share this hashtag **#My7Years** as you are reading this book and as you begin to decree and declare what your 7 years of abundance will look like.

Connect with us!

I would like to hear from you and your wonderful testimony from this book. You can email us at admin@carolynganderson.com or to join our Mailing List text DrCarolyn to 22828

Learn more about other products and services or for booking at **www.carolynganderson.com**

Like our Page
www.facebook.com/DrCarolynAnd

Follow us at: www.twitter.com/DrCarolynAnd

Other Books by Carolyn G. Anderson

Pregnant with a Promise

Focus & Get Results

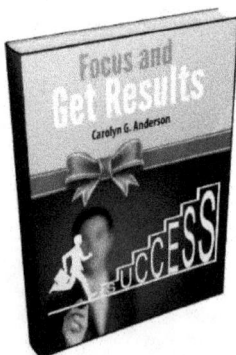

New in 2017

Heal-thy LiFE

Heal-thy Land

Living a Wealthy LiFE on Purpose

Lead-er-SHIP

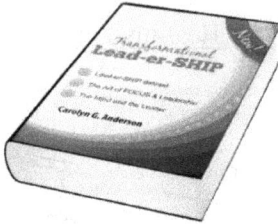

What Happens When the Dream Dies?

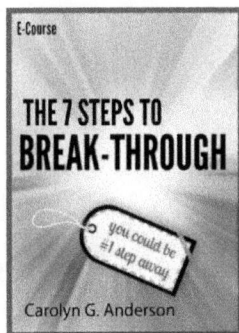

Future Books

#My7Year Series

5778 - 2018 - Book 2
5779 - 2019 - Book 3
5780 - 2020 - Book 4
5781 - 2021 - Book 5
5782 - 2022 - Book 6
5783 - 2023 - Book 7

www.ingramcontent.com/pod-product-compliance
Lightning Source LLC
Chambersburg PA
CBHW060518030426
42337CB00015B/1937